Lucia M. Marvin
N.Y.C. 11/10/61

Between the Lines

LONDON : HUMPHREY MILFORD
OXFORD UNIVERSITY PRESS

BETWEEN THE LINES

By H. M. Tomlinson

Cambridge:

Harvard University Press

1930

First Trade Edition

PRINTED AT THE HARVARD UNIVERSITY PRESS
CAMBRIDGE, MASSACHUSETTS, U.S.A.

THE ADDRESS PRINTED IN THE FOLLOWING PAGES WAS DELIVERED AT PRINCETON UNIVERSITY, YALE UNIVERSITY, D'YOUVILLE COLLEGE, CORNELL UNIVERSITY, AND COLUMBIA UNIVERSITY; AND, IN ITS PRESENT FORM, TO MEMBERS OF THE HARVARD UNION ON OCTOBER 14, 1927

Between the Lines

MR. CHAIRMAN, AND GENTLEMEN:

I SHOULD HAVE BEEN blind had I not noticed, while this morning I was being guided through the buildings of your famous university, that one was announced to speak here to-night whom you were pleased to call a "second Conrad." He will not object to that; and Joseph Conrad cannot. But the compliment made me reminiscent. Here, I thought, is Harvard. Concord, Massachusetts, must be near. In fact, I was actually shown here the rooms once occupied by Emerson, and my guide cannot have known my immediate concern; which I did not show, I hope, for in those apartments there was need for due humility before another of Harvard's famous sons, who now occupies them. Yet I will confess to you that before I was twenty I was familiar with all Emerson's work. I felt his nudge. And that gave me a further thought. There was a greater teacher than Emerson, and to him I came but a little later. There was a man named Thoreau. I put him with Melville and Whitman, and I could hardly say more than that, except that, when young, I carried his *Walden* about in my pocket, as did many young Englishmen then, for the revolt against imperialism and materialism already had definitely arisen in England — nearly forty years ago you will note — and Thoreau was in part responsible for it, strange though that may seem to you. And there you have it. I have reason to doubt that what I have to tell you to-night came from Cracow — from Poland; it came from nearer Concord, not far from here. I myself think that to-night I shall be returning to you something which, I suspect, originated here long before I knew precisely where Harvard was situate. I venture to hint that you Americans should lay claim to a little credit for the inspiration of your remarkable writers of the 'fifties.

My business now is to be candid about the art and craft of letters; I have to confess what literature means to me. A confession is without value unless it be given without reserve. It is sometimes asked of a man whose positive manner is the chief sign of his wisdom: "Well, anyway, what do you know about it?" A formidable question, when we would be honest, and when a chief lesson from one's years is that things are not so simple as one used to think them. There is a drawback — it is not the only drawback — to overcoming one's youth: one feels more and more that things are not so simple as once they appeared to be, and that lessens one's confidence. So please do not pose me with what I know about it all — not with sharp abruptness. The truth is, I have occasionally wondered in secret over the mystery of poetry, I have speculated as to how and why the wheels go round; and I cannot declare that I have arrived at an answer full-orbed and completely satisfactory. In spite of our biological, psychological, and physical laboratories, a few of life's mysteries remain reluctant. Luckily for me as a literary critic — for I also have been paid good money for reviewing literature, or anyhow, for reviewing books — no curious child has ever held me up with a blunt question as to the mysterious turning of the wheels. How and why do they go round? We will omit the additional question of the cynic: Need they go round? For continue to revolve they certainly will.

Don't suppose for a moment that I shall

dare here to attempt to solve the problem. There is a promise to the pure in heart that they shall see God, but there is none made to the man who says he is going to see Him. For what is Art? Tolstoy asked that question, and answered it to his own satisfaction. Others have demurred to his solution. Not many of us, very likely, could do so very much better than Tolstoy, when developing a solution of the components of truth and beauty. A well-known English literary critic, so much of this generation as to be a boy beside Quiller-Couch, Saintsbury, and Gosse, told me one day that he thought all literary criticism could come down to the injunction: "Consider the lilies of the field." That intellectual, that day, was in one of his less critical moods, induced probably by idleness in fine weather in the country. And I do not introduce him here to prove anything, but only to allow him to hint, as I guess the strange words he quoted may hint, that the Epicureanism of these latter days, our cleverest and deadliest cynicism, our light frivolity with what our fathers thought were verities, may be but the consequence of a lowered vitality. Our interest is no longer vital, but is that of the connoisseur. We find it easy to deride; we taste and analyse, and thus we unconsciously admit that the power of our creativeness is past. We are rather tired on the descending slope of our culture. We cannot imagine, for instance, the assurance of Händel's music coming through the capacity for comic insolence of a jazz band. When we are positive, it is usually because of a doubt. We have no doubt about our doubts. The jazz band with its caterwauling saxophones quite harmonizes with things as they are. It expresses youthful abandon and derision, and it does so with the gaiety which I noticed was not unusual with intelligent young men when they greeted the horror of the front line in France, from which they knew they could not escape.

And the feeling to-day seems fairly general that, though the cheat in the compulsion of our materialistic society is plainly manifest, and that few of us are unaware of it, yet nothing can be done about it. There is less chance of escape for us than there was for the soldier in the old front line. The war was certain to end some day, but he would be a bold man who would hint a period to the dominion of the money-power, of the rule of Mammon. That being so, the young, for the most part, say what they think of it with the blare of a saxophone. It is rare for young people to admire Mammon, though worship of a brute god may be a worthy convention, to which they must conform if they would be thought respectable. Useless, then, to expect better music. And again, in any case, there are the clever doubters and the cynics; with the ironic banter of their unbelief they have intimidated us. That was a simple job for them, because it is not easy to answer them. And when innocent but dubious worshippers see our cleverer and bolder young men hitting the solemn gods in our temples over the pate with amusing bladders, deriding those conventional sanctities which society has set up, the show may be said to be over, to all intents and purposes. Industrial society will continue — no doubt about that — but the gods to which it once appealed for its justification now look like the plaster busts, chipped and forlorn, of Victorian notabilities. Our irreverent young people jam a discarded bowler hat at a saucy angle on the dusty head of grandfather's memorial bust, on their way to the mocking cacophony of their dance music. That is my reading of the message of "Ulysses" to us, when James

Joyce maps his journey. That is where we are now: James Joyce and jazz. The message of young genius to-day to us is that there is nothing in it all; that it is not worth while, and that one may as well be ribald and stick out his tongue in a noteworthy manner as do anything else. Not so, we sadly see, did the masterpieces arise. Not thus was established our august though outworn tradition. Not in that spirit of light and derisive impudence did Swift tell us what he thought of our ways. You cannot do polemical prose like Swift's, let it be hinted, nor like Shaw's, without positive conviction moved by passion. And, somehow, we have lost our positive convictions, and so feel no passion. The modern mind, it may be said, apart from poetry and music, has not a few positive convictions, but they are concerned almost solely with the perfecting of machinery and the organization of material forces. There we certainly are much in advance of the ancients. Beethoven could not fly the Atlantic, and sometimes we can, with luck. We are entitled to that distinction and satisfaction. And Keats, I suppose, in these days would fail to get into our more precious and sophisticated publications, for his lyrical emotion would seem spontaneous, innocent, and foolish beside, let us say, the deadly wit of Mr. T. S. Eliot's hopeless *Hollow Men* and *Waste Land*. And certainly the popular journals would reject Keats on immediate printed forms. It was in one of your own bright American journals that once I saw a picture showing the office of a theatrical manager, whose rings and diamond pin competed with the electric lights, whose feet were on his desk, and about whom, on the walls, were choice portraits of dangerous ladies. He was scrutinizing a manuscript just brought to him — the messenger and author stood behind him, and I thought I recognized the shadow of one who had once known Stratford-on-Avon. The manuscript was Hamlet. And the astounded theatrical manager was exclaiming: "What the hell!"

That manager was perfectly right. He was what a shareholder would call a sound manager. For it is certain that your attitude and mine to Art, with that of the theatrical manager, are of first importance. The way we regard it is of the deepest significance. It betrays our day. And so I cannot help thinking that, we being what we are, and the world for which the theatrical manager caters what it is, we might just as well expect the advent of an announcing angel as anything again of the nature of the Ninth Symphony. The Magic Flute is mute. The factory syren has silenced it. And Mr. Eliot, a scholar and poet, genuinely dismayed by the blare of modern life, shrinks from us, and retreats without joy to a seclusion with the strict letter of a nobler tradition, now dead.

Two people, as you know, go to the making of a poem — the poet and the reader. The ray of light becomes visible, we will say, only when an object receives it. The reader who is illuminated is, in a real sense, the poem. The poet and the response live together in the same world and breathe the same air. Now, I ask you, is there that in the prospect of things as they are, in our modern intense preoccupation with the organization of machinery, to move a poet to praise his God? Would not his lyrical joy surprise us? It would be ridiculous to ask us to rhapsodize. So it is likely that we are now getting just what we deserve in the way of art; what we get is no more than the consequence of our worship of a popular god. For undoubtedly a poet is the creature of his time, though he speak forward to a time not his. It is true that

Shakespeare's plays were written because there happened to be a fellow who could write them; yet again, they were written because they were wanted. They were the crowning flower of the extravagant and exploring spirit of that age. And I am aware that the book containing Keats' finest poems took twenty-five years to sell five hundred copies; nevertheless, look back to his time, and consider what poets were busy then. Something then was stirring, evidently, which has failed since. Very likely we do not understand the poet when we have him, but at least we do not even have him unless ours is an age in which music will make men look up, as though they knew what it was, and were glad.

So as to this problem of literature, why the wheels turn, and how they should turn when the motive comes, I don't think we need bother too much as to the "how" of it. That is the problem of style, and the problem of style may be left to whoever has something to say. But from what source is great art derived? That is the question of real importance. For obviously the time may come when the Pierian spring may cease; Pegasus may be seen no more. And we may have many inventions, and men able to concoct gases which, though in minute quantities, will destroy the greater number of the people of a city; and we may be able to fly the ocean in order to perform so meritorious an act; and the greatness of our imports and exports may cause us to smile at the poverty of folk in less fortunate ages and places; nevertheless, there may be one or two things of which we shall be deprived because these other great benefits have been added to us, and their absence may make all the difference to our peace of mind. Yet we shall never know why we are not at peace, but remain desultory, restless, and out of accord with the seasons. And the men who could tell us why will be precisely the men, whose lives and work challenge our day, to whom we do not, as a rule, think it worth while to listen. Outsiders, those fellows. Men of no consequence, because the signs that they are successful are by no means plain. For like the people who once stoned the prophets, and killed those who were sent unto them, we are never likely to listen to the words which are strangely not in harmony with the things we want to hear, and a success which cannot be measured by the accepted standard will be failure to us. We want to hear, chiefly, whatever comforts our prejudices, justifies our conventions, and confirms us in the pursuit of the things we desire.

It would be quite fair if you asked me here: If that is your faith, then why go on? Even good men would take to drugs, with that outlook, and it seems enough to make them. Quite right. Yet it is perfectly natural for a man to go on talking, though his words are about as congenial as Jeremiah's. It is n't that he cannot stop it. But he is sustained by the hope that there are more people in the world than might be thought who regard things as they are much as he does himself. He does n't like them, and he trusts others do not. It is surprising how often the challenging comment on the accustomed ways of the world happens to be just the word that people were waiting to hear. That is of happy augury for young men and women, who are secretly in revolt against the hard, material aspect of their age. Only let them own up cheerfully, and they will hear responsive halloos from everywhere in the surrounding darkness. They will find they are by no means alone. And because of those young people I will admit a further belief that this mechanical age with its faith in the immortality of machinery, and the eternal output of the engines — to doubt which is the new blasphemy — has in it now the promise of something different and better. Their revolt, for instance, is in it, though unvoiced. I for one have not yet got to the stage of regarding the universe as a silly joke, and this earth as a stage on which man, in the process of his evolution, at last shall commit hara-kiri as the logical consequence of his own ingenuity. You know, there is not much in a great joke at which there is nobody to laugh, not even a god.

There was a time — we will call it before the war — when whatever motived society, whatever compelled men to be busy, was accepted by the more intelligent junior members of the family at least with stoicism. They must have thought, I guess, that though it all seemed rather foolish and empty, yet who were they to question it? They did not question it. When their turn came, they began to perform their parts, as their forefathers had done; and they neither questioned nor complained. But, like it or lump it, the war made a difference. I will speak for a bit of Europe, at least; the war made a revolution. It very definitely displayed in Europe the reality under those polite and smooth appearances of society which till then the young had never questioned. Now they know what is in the family vault. No wonder they cannot sing the old songs! No wonder, as there seems to be no escape, they regard the saxophone an expressive instrument! No wonder they think there is no need to look anywhere for the truth about life but in the biological laboratory! No wonder they look upon such an elder as myself, who actually mentions Händel and Beethoven — and may even let the name of Dickens slip, by inadvertence, before he is done — as a sentimentalist! They accept life as inevitable instinctive movements to specified promptings — they see no other way in which to regard it — and may be said to go into their fathers' business, to keep the city running, not because they like it, or believe in it, not out of any conviction that it is something well worth doing, but because it does n't matter; and they go in a spirit of buoyant and freely expressed cynicism. And I don't blame them. It would not matter if I did, for they need only turn to the world about them, point at something there, and smile at me without saying a word.

What has this to do, you will ask, with the way I look at literature? Everything, it seems to me. Let us suppose that the curious infant with its poser about the turning of the wheels is here. The child has put the question to us. How are we to answer it? I will assume that in any case we all regard the problem of literature to be important, as the matter of Prohibition is important, and the danger of radicalism, and whether or not our breakfast food has enough calories.

Then let me, for one, own up. I see no essential difference between Isaiah and Swift as men with something to say to us. I am unable, I mean, to separate religion and literature. For me they are the same. The writer who would give his public what it wants, with his tongue in his cheek, is in the same class exactly as the other fellow who once took pieces of silver in payment for treachery. He denies the light. And whether the public wants what we have to say has nothing to do with it. Perhaps the public is a good judge; perhaps the public realizes that there is precious little in what we have to say; and so neglects us, quite properly. That is for the poet to discover for himself; and discovery will depend on the depth and selflessness of his convictions and on his courage. For if a man wilfully chooses literature, then let him take a trial run on locusts and wild honey, to see whether or not he can stand it. I need not remind you that there is no need to worry about a diet of locusts if you are going to trim green hats, because there is a plenteous demand for that sort of delectable millinery. But I am not talking, I know, to aspirant milliners, eager for the sweet rewards of trimming. I do not say that a young poet should solemnly survey himself to see how he looks in goatskins, and wonder whether he will fit the wilderness as well as St. John. A deliberate choice of the wilderness, because of the intense conviction of a poet that he is a forerunner, argues something either very big or quite mad. It is not always easy to tell which. But we can safely leave such fellows to look after themselves. They would n't give a locust for what we think about it. I am merely addressing those who may choose the work to do which came my way, and are not unwilling to listen to the opinions of one who has spent some years upon it. We know that two people go to the making of a poem. The poet's word, somehow, has in it something more than the writer expressed. So there is just a possibility — my only excuse for addressing you — that a chance word of mine may be seen to have in it more than I meant by it; something beyond it, and better. For that is the way of a word — it grows — and its author is not altogether responsible. Here is the place to admit that nothing in the way of reading matter surprises me more than the quotations which reviewers lift from my own work. So that is what they see in it! I always read those quotations as though they were no concern of mine. They are mine only when they are bad examples of English, and therefore sterile. If they are good, then they are translated; they are out of my control; mine no longer; a reader sees in them something I never saw, and he is already beyond me with them.

You see, I am not talking of technique, of style. I have read very many books on that subject, and shall read more, I suppose, held to that task by wonder and hope ever renewed, though to the end I fear I shall make nothing of it. That is not the fault of the analytical critics. At one time I imagined it was but the fault of a horny cranium which, if arduously polished, would at length admit the light; but there has been no luck. So though I shall continue to study, off and on, by what ordering of rhythms, forms, colours, words, and sounds, magic is made, and truth and beauty are compelled, the clue by which all these elements are resolved is one that I expect to learn on the morning when the Last Trump is heard, and the Veil is rent.

You remember that Tolstoy, when the critics were describing him as the greatest writer since Shakespeare, came in from his oxen and his cornfields, read such praise, and wrote in his diary, "Now what do they mean by that?" I wish he himself had tried to shape an answer to his question by writing down all the probabilities, even when they were ridiculous. But he was much too interested in his farming, and in writing *War and Peace* as relaxation after ploughing.

It was ever so. The men who might be able to tell us how it is done are always so busy doing it that our anxiety to learn the way of the trick is rarely known to them, and appears not to interest them. Chehov, who was aware that we should like to be let into the secret, used to be amused by questioners, and declared modestly that he knew nothing about it, and did not believe it was worth troubling over; meaning by that, I suppose, that the difficulty was like the one we have over good and evil, and the reason we are born, and why toads have no feathers. All very well for Chehov, but like others of his kind, he forgot that he himself had no need to bother about the way it should be done; he could do it.

It is easy to speculate about the problem of style. Everyone here could do that and perhaps does it. It is like discussing the problem of immortality; the evidence may be assorted, as usual, according to what we desire to find, and all the evidence which does not accord with our predilections may be ruled out, very reasonably, as irrelevant. I must say, as a literary critic, that though there may be absolute criteria for the judging of books, I do not know them and so cannot submit any. A learned critic may somehow manage to convey an impression that, like a chemist, he has an array of apparatus of which every item has its specific purpose, and that his measuring is done by impersonal scales which never fail to distinguish the just from the unjust. Yet we need not believe him, unless we want to.

But I should be sorry if you thought that in this I have dismissed good taste with the evidence which is irrelevant because we do not like it; or that good taste may be got like any other pleasing commodity, and added, when necessary — as an afterthought, may be — to reduce the asperities of a harsh compound of scholarship, or to disguise the worst crudities that arise from a sudden influx of money. Good taste, probably, is our taste, or how should we know it to be good? We will swear, nevertheless, that however we may define good taste, yet it is not merely a bland yet noticeable polish added to an idiosyncrasy. We suspect it may be something in the grain. Let us suppose — for there is no reason why all illusions should do us harm —that good taste gets its virtue from those clouds of glory which, so Wordsworth assures us, the lucky ones brought with them. Some people are not, it appears, entirely forgetful.

We will admit, then, that good taste is not something we may obtain at school, if studious, or may cultivate as a hobby. It does not necessarily follow from success in other things. Whatever it is, it gives to those who have it confidence for which, often enough, we see no reason in nature. They are quite enthusiastic, at times, about the quality of a book, a picture, or an oriental rug, when we know of nothing to say. Whether or not there are absolute criteria for the judging of literature, or of music, or of any art apart from its technicalities, we need, I think, make no mistake about one thing. Art is not, as some commentators ask us to believe, a choice and decorative matter set apart for the few who have been initiated into its mysteries, as though it were the cunning collecting of old furniture or antique clocks. If literature were that, if it were not a flowering of life, just as is any rose, then it would be no better than any other indoor game.

But literature is more than that to us. It is more than a pleasing occupation for those who prefer it to golf, or have a nice discrimination in old porcelain. It is not something ornamental to be added to the house when business improves and leisure is won. You and I may be light-hearted in our temple, but we do not find it easy to permit freedom there to the Philistines. Literature and religion have so much in common that we do not separate the psalms of David and songs of Blake, Isaiah and John Bunyan, or St. Paul and Donne. There is a cool but terrible zeal in these writing and religious fanatics—

though that may be little, if uncomfortable to live with; but chiefly there is a passion for truth, which is the same as beauty, or, as some folk prefer to call it, the love of God.

For religion, or, as we will say, literature, is the expression of a human need more compelling than that satisfied by commerce or politics. In the best of poetry, as in music, man is a bit above himself. Once you have been moved by it, once you have been changed by *Moby Dick*, or by a passage of great music, you will find it hard and even dangerous to venture upon a survey of modern life and its native literature. Neither editors nor publishers would like it. We have to lower the standard, and judge contemporary letters on an easier plane. In such days as ours, when respect goes mostly to the signs of material power, we do not look for noble poetry; what is the use of going through to-day's ubiquitous factory in a search for Apollo disguised in blue overalls?

Well, though the governors of our routine and the captains of our industries be as cautious as practical and level-headed people should be, sometimes Apollo, who brings light and music, appears — dressed the same as Bill Jones; and then we had better look out for squalls. For literature is an expression of fundamental life, and won't be denied; at its lowest it is an indication of the health of a nation no less certain than a battle fleet and the statistics that prove increasing trade; at its highest it may put us beyond time and chance. Our traditional institutions may dissolve in its light. Young men may look up from a mere book, and think they have sighted Mount Zion. And men who only think they have sighted that delectable mountain are likely to prove awkward customers.

Because—we are forced to the conclusion —the highest things in Art are outside common experience, and perhaps, as in the case of religion and great music, outside experience altogether. We may discuss them, but that makes no difference to them. When we are lost in an ocean of Händel's music, we cannot tell what it conjures in us; but we do suspect that if, when finished at last with mundane things and we were on our way to Sirius—or wherever it may be we have to go—and heard sounds like that, then they would be all in accord with our new state amid the stars.

What! you expostulate, is the judging of books, as well as the impulse to write, as vague as that? Is that what you call guidance?

I do. What more could we have? For it is certain that whoever will not courageously face the facts of life, whether he likes them or not, will never be able to tell the true from the false in literature. I am convinced that the man who sins against the light; who is a time-server, and prefers comfortable security in seclusion with a bucket over his light, and thus recognizes things as they are, in the long run gets the lie in the soul so much at home that he cannot even tell a good book from a bad one, much less write a good book. After all, such light as we know is not without its uses. Light was probably meant to serve some purpose. In our search for realities we omit it at our peril.

You may have any message you like to give the public, but the essential condition for its delivery is sincerity. Unless a book gets written in the spirit of challenging and fearful levity which once sent some admirable lads "over the wire," then I fail to see why it should be done at all, when so many needful chores are waiting. Let us not deceive ourselves. It is certain that a great writer never worries about his style, that ticklish subject in a course of English for aspirants to journalism, and we see the reason for it. Something else possesses the man. The importance of what he has to say controls him, and his chief anxiety is that we should clearly understand it. If that does not give him style, then nothing can; and if style is there, then it will be in accord with the importance of his message. The closest study of the styles of all the great masters of English will not give us anything of importance to say, any more than wearing Napoleon's old hat would help a modern general to victory. If this seems a hard saying, then let an unbeliever try to write like Swift. A zeal for truth is the spring of art; though it would be useless here to discuss those tests by which we may recognize truth when we suspect it to be about. Perhaps it is a matter of instinct. It is not always easy to see the truth of a matter. I will venture here to use as a test of truth a gigantic object of art which stands near Hyde Park of London. You will find, near St. George's Hospital, a war memorial in the classic form of an immense bronze figure of a youth wearing but a fig-leaf and a huge sword, and you might wonder what it symbolizes. Well, it pretends to be a tribute to the men of the British Machine Gun Corps who fell in the Great War, but on its pedestal you may read these words: "Saul hath slain his thousands, but David his tens of thousands."

Now, the fig-leaf is a silly evasion and a snigger. David was not of the neuter gender, nor was any machine gunner that I ever met; but that inscription, for me, proves the cruelty, the essential ugliness, of the whole conception. David slew his *tens* of thousands! You see? That image is not at all a tribute to the men who fell, as it pretends to be, and as its artist thinks it is. It is the glorification of Carnage. It is a tribute, not to the poor machine gunners who died, but to the Machine Gun itself. It says so, though without conscious intent. Instinctively we worship the machine, in these days. The inscription might just as well have been in German, for certainly most of our own men were slain by the German David. There that testimony, an unconscious falsity in itself, as its inscription shows, stands to Moloch, and not far from Westminster Abbey. Yet, on the other hand, we had an awful row about the ugliness of Epstein's tribute to W. H. Hudson, which is not far from this very David. If you want to know what can happen when, with a lie poisoning the mind, we judge a book or a work of art, there it is. Studious nicety can be shown over the adjustment of a fig-leaf. The harshness of Rima's marble breasts can be most unladylike. But the triumph of a brute god over the young may be noted with grave approval.

Is that unimportant? Everything that matters in literature depends on just such distinctions. If we can find no precise rules for the judging of literature, we see, nevertheless, that on our choice a very great deal depends. We may, and without knowing what we do, deny the light. We may hail for our choice, and again without knowing what we do, Barabbas. For let us note carefully that the choice of Barabbas is also a sincere choice, though woeful. It is entirely the consequence of a genuine and heartfelt preference. And we may be always quite sure that for us to challenge such a choice may prompt immediate, reasonable, and even righteous indignation. We may get stoned with the best. For can it be doubted that an instinctive desire, once it is rationalized, is no longer a desire at all, but an intellectual conception worthy of reasonable men? Well, we never doubt it in the heat of the argument, as the last war proved well enough.

The writing and judging of books may be as important as that to you and to me. But we will not deceive ourselves. There are not many people who really care. For it is a fact that you may say just what you like about literature in public, and yet never raise that intensity of joy or resentment which might come of hinting that a famous statesman had spoken favourably of tinned tomatoes while knowing in his dark heart he preferred them fresh. You may, as a literary critic and in a responsible paper, couple the last popular novel of Miss Jones with Hardy's *Tess*, and even hint to Hardy that time flies, and that the young have all their life before them; and yet the chances are your host of silent readers will fancy there is something shrewd and clever behind such a remark. One feels too sorry to laugh over it. It is funny, we know, to see a dignified fellow-citizen go down on a banana skin. But if such an accident were to be witnessed at all hours of the day and in any street, we might begin to feel at last that some control should be exercised over the banana skins of the irresponsible.

But contemporary literary criticism is spread with those banana skins. Consider the happy abandon with which slippery stuff about books is thrown about nowadays for the unwary—how wonderful is the literature that is issued every week—how great the novels of Miss Jones—how majestic the prose style of Mr. Winston Churchill, the English statesman—and the poetic genius of Mr. Potts! Can it all be true? But if it be ridiculous, as no doubt it is, does it really matter, some may ask?

Does it matter, when it takes America seventy years to learn that in Herman Melville it had a son who was one of its most significant portents since the Declaration of Independence?

For my part, I am sure such bad and indifferent criticism of books is just as serious as a city's careless drainage. Of course it is important, for at least frivolity appears unseemly, and carelessness something worse, about the springs of life and death. Though it may be largely true that our literary criteria are only our personal prejudices elegantly disguised in reasonable argument, yet one does see errors in criticism which ought not to be made by anyone who knows a book from an unpleasant warning. I remember noting, in one important London newspaper, that a certain popular novelist's prose style, though admittedly very bad, was quite all right after all, for was not the prose style of Carlyle also ugly? I gathered that it was the *matter* of a book that was of importance, and not the style.

I must say that any press critic who would make such a primary mistake as that ought to be instantly discharged. The style of *Past and Present* ugly, and not beautiful, though it so perfectly embodies its purpose? Was there ever a good book with a bad style, or an attractive flower with a disgusting smell, or a noble statesman with a dishonest soul? Such fallacies are by no means unimportant, even though our literary standards may be nothing but our personal preferences. Commonly held, they may prove of no less consequence than the cheerful and comprehensive faith that war is inevitable, that all men are liars, that statesmen are great, that admirals and generals are heroes, that self-preservation is the first law of nature, and the other phrases, freely advertised, which we use because they are handy and we cannot be bothered to think them over.

The little things matter, even in books. They are significant. Even the style matters. For style is not ornamentation, nor even, as some people think, when they remember Charles Lamb and Sir Thomas Browne, beautiful ornamentation. Only a bad style can come of artful deliberation, as Oscar Wilde and others have shown. Style depends, first and last, on what a writer has to say, and the kind of man he is. It is not his dress, but the essential man, the man even his friends may not know. We have *Elia* and the *Religio Medici* to prove it. And yet, you have seen, among those critics to whom you must often go for guidance there are some who suppose that a good book can still be ugly — that is to say, that a bad book can be a good one. You may complain, as a correspondent did once to a paper for which I was writing, that these are personal views, as in fact I have confessed, and not objective criticism. Now I will ask you this: What is objective criticism? I wish I knew how to recognize it. I fear it is no better than the objective and fabulous monsters we see when we are a bit unbalanced—we think it is there, but it is not. That is the reason why there is no perfect and objective style, and no absolute and impersonal criteria by which literature may be judged as a thing in itself. Style is good or bad according to the spirit which forms it. Good style is more than the use of the right words in the right order, if by right words we mean technical exactitude, and not that indefinable appeal which is in the form, colour, and poise of a daffodil when the light favours it. There it is, simply, when it is done.

All very well, that, you exclaim, but how is it to help me? How are such airy ideas to be worked into the order of my studies? The fact is, I do not know how it can help you. More likely it may worry you. That is your affair. But remember that a man is never more alone than when he has to resolve something of the first importance to himself. You have to set your own course, steer your ship by what stars you know, and see to it that your lights are burning bright; and if you notice, with no joy, that your friends are on slightly divergent courses, which will take them out of sight before nightfall, wish them Godspeed.

That suggests loneliness. It does not hint at an easy and profitable familiarity with editors and publishers. The thought occurs to you: How am I to know, when alone, that assuredly I shall reach port?

You won't know. That fact has to be faced. If a man would prefer less risk, and more assurance with careful industry of making the right landfall with a profitable cargo, let him try Wall Street or an automobile works. With such an end in view he could hardly miss port, if he determines to make it.

Literature is different. It is not a profession, if we mean by that a means to food and shelter. It is, in a vital sense, a profession of faith; and it is well known that a man's faith evades every new concrete image to which he would reduce it. The most we can say of his faith is that it is expressed in his work, if his work so interests us that we attach importance to its implications.

Let me attempt to show that these abstractions are not, after all, so ghostly and futile as I may have suggested, through sheer clumsiness in a difficulty. May I tell you that I have been greatly impressed, surprised, and disturbed by Manhattan? Your city of New York is, I think, the most beautiful and awe-inspiring city in the world. It is like no other city on earth. Immense and majestic, it is superior to every effort of one of its admirers, or one of its victims, to image what it inspires in them. New York moves one even to terror; sometimes an observer sees in its sheer precipices and towers a hint that man in his inventive audacity is overdoing his part. He feels that if ever the jealous gods, waking from a long sleep, happen to catch sight of Manhattan, it had better watch the heavens. Its magnitude and its serene and haughty confidence in its destiny are challenging. And may I say also that I do not feel a foreigner when walking in Fifth Avenue? I feel quite at home there. I can enjoy myself all day loafing about Downtown. For me the American scene is a prolongation of my own heritage; I feel in no way an alien here; yet I do feel alarm, when I see the prospect of New York from some angles. New York is the latest expression of that industrial and utterly material society, crazy over machinery and the scientific management of forces to profitable ends, which began with a steam-engine and ended — so far as common faith in its righteousness in England is concerned — in bombs on Piccadilly. And is it to that end, or an end something like it, we may fairly ask, that modern man is heading with all his ingenuity and energy? If not, where is he going? Does he know?

He does not know. And he does n't appear to want to know. He is engaged in a grand adventure, but he has no idea of the way it may end — though now and then, in a quiet moment, he hesitates, and is susceptible to a little wholesome fear. To what all this material wealth and power will take him he does not know and nobody can tell him. As a friend of mine, a man of letters, and a New Yorker, said to me in his own city only on Sunday last: "These powers are loose —

they are in charge now — we do not control them, they control us. We set them going, and now they keep us going. There is nothing we can do about it. Sometimes the city is so wonderful that I want to cheer it, and sometimes it scares me. But what I feel makes no difference to what it is and what it must be. There it is, and nothing we can do can alter it."

I tell you I don't agree with him. That is the fatalism with which the Orient regards its days and nights. I have spoken to many Americans, most of them young people, and I have the distinct impression that they feel any vast modern city, with its inspiriting yet disturbing ascendency, is inimical. It symbolizes the way all the world appears to be going, and they do not like it — nobody of courage cares to feel that his soul is drifting willy-nilly with a flood of instinctive humanity. "Dear city of Cecrops," they whisper, being shy, these young people, "but shall we not say, 'Dear city of Zeus'?"

Why not? Is it not true that even gigantic and wealthy New York is but the outer show of its people's commonest opinions and desires? So how if their thoughts should veer? We change our thoughts and change our world. And that is the task of the poet, to persuade his fellows to pause and to look up to the everlasting hills. I would back the young poets of America against all New York, were they in revolt against it, no matter what its majesty and aspect of power. They could, in the end, give it a spirit which it has not, if perchance they have heard of a better word, and have the courage to let their fellows know it.

As the story goes, Dagon fell. Never believe it. If he did, it is not so very noticeable. He is, in fact, very firm upon his throne. Yet every poet, and every good reader, must believe in his heart that some day the ugliness which is supreme shall be laid low. What other reason can there be to make us cheerful and hopeful at our tasks?

DATE DUE

GAYLORD PRINTED IN U.S.A.